Amazing Pictures and Facts About Brazil

By: Mina Kelly

Introduction

Historians believe that people began living in Brazil nearly 32,000 years ago! Brazil is home to diverse culture with a very rich religious, culinary, and musical history. Let's explore Brazil!

What is the Official Name of Brazil?

The Federative Republic of Brazil is the official name of the country. However, most of the world refers to it as Brazil. The name of the country may also be written as Republica Federativa do Brasil or Brasil.

Where is Brazil Located?

Brazil is located in Eastern South America. The country is bordered by ten other countries: Argentina, Bolivia, Colombia, French Guiana, Guyana, Paraguay, Peru, Suriname, Uruguay, and Venezuela.

What is the Geography Like in Brazil?

Brazil has thick rain forests in the northern region. There are also mountains, hills and rolling plains in other areas of the country. Brazil has a large coastline bordering the Atlantic Ocean.

How Big is Brazil?

Brazil is the fifth largest country in the world! It has an estimated population of 209 million people in 2016. The country itself is a little bit smaller than the United States of America, with 3.29 million square miles of land (8.51 million square km).

What is the Climate Like in Brazil?

The climate of Brazil is tropical and humid. There are some subtropical areas; this means that the air is not so humid, but still very warm.

Does Brazil Have a Famous Landmark?

Yes, the most famous landmark in Brazil is located in Rio de Janeiro. The landmark is a statue of Christ called, "Christ the Redeemer." This statue is located at the top of Corcovado Mountain and overlooks the city.

What is the Flag of Brazil Like?

The flag of Brazil has a green background, with a yellow rhombus and then a blue circle inside of the rhombus. Inside the blue circle is a starry sky and the motto, "Ordem e Progresso" (Order and Progress). The starry sky has 27 five pointed stars that represent individual states within the country.

What is the Capital of Brazil?

The capital of Brazil is called Brasilia. Although Brasilia is the capital, it is not the largest city. Sao Paulo is the largest city in population.

What is the National Flower of Brazil?

The national flower of Brazil is called the Ipe-amarelo or Tecoma chrysostricha. These are bright yellow flowers that grow on trees in the spring time.

Are the Summer Olympics in Brazil?

Yes! In the summer of 2016 the Olympic Games will be in Rio de Janeiro, Brazil. Rio is the first South American city to host the summer games, ever!

What is Life Like in Brazil?

Most Brazilians live near cities or the coast. Family structure and values are important to the Brazilian people; they are usually quite large too.

What do People Eat in Brazil?

The food in Brazil is a combination of many cultures. Brazilian food uses tropical fruits, fish, meat, rice, beans and much more! A popular dish in Brazil is called feijoada, a stew with beans and pork.

What is the Government of Brazil?

The government of Brazil is known as a Democratic Federal Republic. Brazil has a president that is elected by its people for a four year term. Below the president are a federal senate and a chamber of deputies.

What is the Main Religion in Brazil?

Brazilian people are very religious, it is estimated that 90% of people have a religious ideal. About three quarters of the people in Brazil identify as Roman-Catholic. Other Christian religions are also quite popular.

What are the Main Exports of Brazil?

The top exports of Brazil in the year 2015 included: oil seed, ores, oil, meat, machines, vehicles, iron, steel, sugar, coffee, tea, and spices. The goods exported from Brazil in 2015 earned the country approximately $191.1 billion (U.S. Dollars)!

What is the Most Popular Sport in Brazil?

The most popular sport in Brazil is football (soccer). The Brazilian national team has won the World Cup five times! They are considered to be one of the most successful teams ever.

What is the Brazilian Coat of Arms?

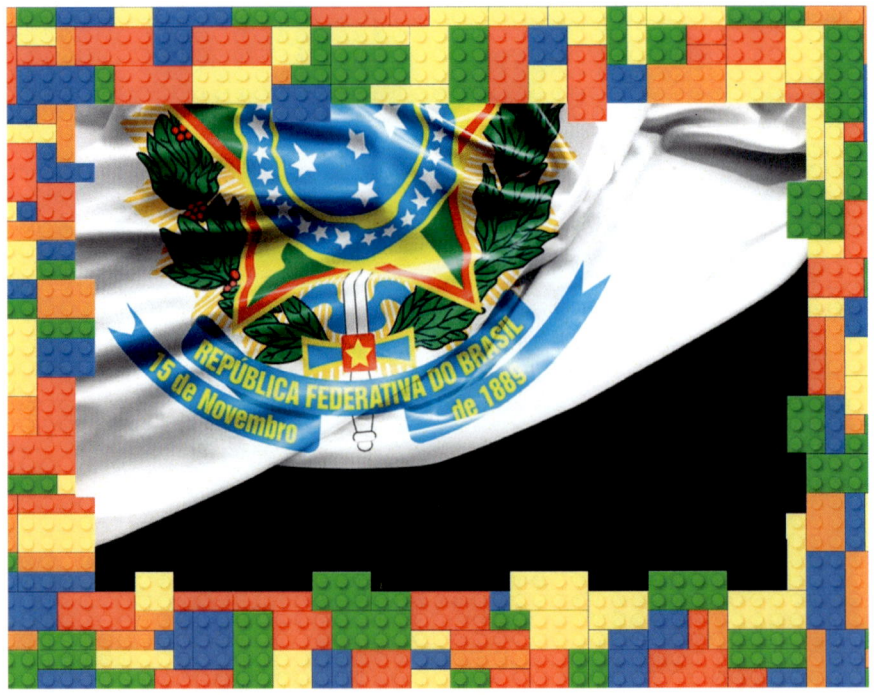

A coat of arms is a symbol unique to a country or family. The Brazilian coat of arms is a design that has several similar features of the Brazilian flag (the stars and colors). However, it also has unique things added to it, such as a coffee plant, tobacco plant and the Southern Cross.

Does Brazil Have a Rainforest?

Yes! Brazil is home to the Amazon rainforest. Brazil has approximately 1/3 of the world's rainforest. Amazingly, it also has the most diverse species of plants and animals in the world.

What is the Official Language of Brazil?

The official language of Brazil is called Portuguese. Portuguese spoken in Brazil is often different than Portuguese spoken in Portugal. What language do you speak in your country?

What is the Amazon River?

The Amazon River is the second longest river in the world. Did you know it is 4,000 miles (6400 km) long? The Amazon River runs through most of South America, including Brazil.

Made in the USA
San Bernardino, CA
14 April 2017